THE LIVING AIR

THE LIVING AIR

MASIELA LUSHA

BLAZEVOX[BOOKS]
Buffalo, New York

The Living Air
by Masiela Lusha
Copyright © 2016

Published by BlazeVOX [books]

Printed in the United States of America

Interior design and typesetting by Geoffrey Gatza
Cover Art by Fadil Berisha

First Edition
ISBN: 978-1-60964-271-6
Library of Congress Control Number: 2016937146

BlazeVOX [books]
131 Euclid Ave
Kenmore, NY 14217

Editor@blazevox.org

publisher of weird little books

BlazeVOX [books]

blazevox.org

21 20 19 18 17 16 15 14 13 12 01 02 03 04 05 06 07 08 09 10

BlazeVOX

BlazeVOX

Acknowledgements

We are the sum of our dearest friends and passing acquaintances. I would like to thank the force of people who have guided, inspired, and built dreams alongside my own. You've left an enduring space wider than you can imagine.

I would especially like to dedicate this book to you, the reader. Each line is thoughtfully crafted for your valued time. My single desire is to inspire you, and nourish the deepest bends of your muse and self-reflection. You are in every word of this book.

I would like to thank my wonderful editor, *Geoffrey Gatza* at BlazeVOX publishing: Your sheer kindness and belief in my craft nourished an essential courage in my creativity. You have been the force in realizing this dream, and in acknowledging my possibilities as a poet. Thank you for standing as an example, and for inspiring me through your own incredible work.

Fadil Berisha: While your humble spirit will not allow any credit for my career, I feel honored to consider you my friend and mentor. Your generosity in our society, your safe space for creative souls, and your ready hand for guidance has left an indelible mark in me; I see you, and I will always strive to meet your benevolence and kindness.

Bruce Helford: How can I complete any project without a quite reflection on your mentorship throughout my career? You've single-handedly elevated my career to a level I could not imagine, and believed in me through every chapter; to say I owe my success to you is simply an understatement. Thank you for motivating me throughout our decades of friendship, and for defining the art and grace of a true leader. A leader nourishes confidence in others, and inspires excellence through example. Thank you for standing as my example.

My mother, Daniela: What can I express on this page that you have not heard many times before? Your tireless drive for lifelong dreams, your passion for all things beautiful and creative, and your unapologetic pursuit to love and nourish is the bedrock of my existence. I owe all my poems to you; you have defined my muse to live and love.

Ramzi, my husband: We've crafted quite a world together. I love you, and feel honored to call you my best friend. Your heart and dignity is truly unmatched. You remain my greatest inspiration of all.

For my husband,
who always inspires.

For my mother,
who always believes.

THE LIVING AIR

Poets

We stalk the truth

As poets

Sensualists—
A duality—
Limited in sanity.

We labor in our muse.
Carving alphabets
Of experience
Into our hearts.

Bound in primal longings,
We pine to be understood
By ourselves.

As poets,

Our lamentations are glorious,
filled with the virtues angels
would learn to envy.

We fall in love forever
Many times, and many times

We die.

Circe

Circe—One body
Of moving sea
A shattered tide leads you home.
One wind to own your will
And shift your value into swine.

She holds your loyalty in her accord;
Your anchors are bubbles against her rage.
She is Circe— the goddess,
Shining her truth before your eyes
Shining her sorcery onto your ship
Of journeys.

She embraces you as prisoners
And releases you as learners—

She is Circe, your sorceress
Of Woman and Tides.

Muse

In other words: to exist.

Sincerely.

To dress the night and live
And search the very breadth
Of language—to seek and marvel
To disagree and open
The clarities. To ponder
The lyrics. To re-invite
Insanities, to shine
Against the weak.

To sing—

To bubble inside one's other half
And to measure one's growth
In poetry of reason—

To muse, muse,
Until its rhyme

Is recalled, rewritten
And one might even say then:

To muse is to live
And die in the spirit of words;
Never to dream, never to silence
And pluck petals in meditation

Humming wisdom
        Listened by stone-etched stars.

Medusa's Wisdom

It is the wisest craft of rebirth:
A union of illusion's dualities:
One birth, one death of course--

The planes of immortality
Devoured by her tusks of knowledge
On our eventual demise;

It is the truth we muse away from to escape;
But a binding to our fates, nonetheless.
Our treasures as men and women
Alike. Yes, she is a woman, but she is fair

In her game of transformations—
A liberating truth that through death
        We return, reborn.

Eternal Love

> *Meditation upon a photograph of two skeletal remains wrapped in their final embrace*

Your passions are asleep now,
Entangled in the mass of nights,
Beneath the sheets of hours,
Inside the braids of your companion.

Sleep now.

Sleep inside your wonders,
And ossify your place
Inside our muse.

Rest within our illustrations
Of eternal truth.

The night is patient
For your return,
When you

Rise

Through words,

And take the hand of your beloved.

Ten little bones
Embrace, grip and kiss
For the eternal relief of love,

The little temperament
Of your affections

Can only rise,

> Rise.

Hawai'i

In the thickening distance
A red blush calms and reels.

Before me, the quilted sea
Trembles into an awakening,
Into raw, inexorable dance.

I rise before you.

Tender statue, perennial promise
Of whispering palms and rising wind,
Sinking as your body of dreams,

Vast in its shining glory,
Calling remembrance,
Calling all that was, all that will remain
All that softened
Into a tender,
       indelible dream.

Kumari Devi

*The living goddess. In Nepal, Kumari Devi is the tradition
of worshiping pre-pubescent girls as manifestations of the divine
female energy in Hindu religious traditions.*

Lead her; teach her
To draw this tantric sacrifice--
It is another form of offering
like her own, in which she gives--
unknowingly from perfection and youth.

Kumari Devi will not fear this darkness
All darkness; it is her cave
of new worship and jewels:
*It is a test, dear child, to weigh
your divinity.*

Teach her to float upon this earth
Within her palace of prayers,
for her feet have discovered
the bareness of idolization.

Teach her not to cry,
to whimper before the king--
before her adopted people,
never to rub her eyes before
her children.
Her pearly drops (valued
by mother) are cause for alarm;
calling the voice of death
Before her painted eye
just between her
Two dilating windows into another realm.

Grip her hand and kiss her cheek,
This pale child needs reason to believe
Her blood is valued
Outside the walls of her divinity.

We Are the Mob

We are the mob,
We are your family,
Your gods,

The words that stitch your fate,
The sighs, the sounds, the fiery lips
The fists. We are your loyalties,
The mending of your faith.

We are your forgiver,
Your intruder,
The canvas of your taste.

And you.

You are
Our servant,
Our neighbor,
Our enemy,

Our friendly prayer
Before the feast.

One More

Here is one more letter from one poet
To the poet feasting in you.
One more frame of nature
One more touch of symmetry
One notation of humanity.
One measure of wisdom
Rounding your lips
As the reader...

Here is one more disguise,
One mask of philosophy—

One more actor speaking one more line.

Here is one more truth
        And one more lie.

Ode to Mother

Two angels

Play & in their rosy chamber
They weigh your name
Like rhyming treasures:

"If there were a word, mightier
Than Love,

'Mother'

Would be mightier,
And far more loyal.

And if a single word
Can command from Kings

A pause or tear, what word
Is greater, & far more dear?'"

"A word loftier
Than that humble praise,"

The other angel plays.

"'Fate'

Hangs high above
This cradle in which we stir,
And concurs all kings, both vile
And sincere. Fate concurs all,

'Fate' is the word."

"Fate may steer
Happiness we bestow,
Thus I bow

With respect
For your word.

But can this 'fate' collapse
Three allied gods

Of love,
And moral dynasty?

Can this word you hold so dear,
Quake immortality
With windward fears?

'Mother' can combat
This splintered shadow,
My word is armed with love.

'Fate' can breed & die with work,
But love is the child of mother.
And mother is saved by child.
As mother cradles
The child in youth,
The child shines her name
With proof…

Above the 'fated'
Eclipse of death.

This vital truth of 'Mother'
Weighs far greater
Than the common
Mapping of your stars.

This humble praise
I pronounce:
'Mother'

Hugs your 'fate'
As time hugs the scars."

The other angel stirs:
"Please consider
My word, 'Fate'
Is armed
With much:

Joy, death,
Envy, & a mask
Of love, we draw
As obsessions--

What stirs
My word's work
Is a single measure
Bound to every person,
And even in your child

Of love—

This occasional
Poison we mourn as hate.

My word can command
Such venom, I sadly admit,

Such venom, indeed,

That feasts away
At the tender crafting
Of this nurtured child's faith.

Through my 'fate'

Your product of love

Your cherished child

Has learned to hate.

& if there is no love,
Is there a 'mother'?

If love is to abandon
Your word,
Your word serves mine
Through mortality.

Through my word,
Yours must die.

'Mother' is but folly
To the hidden demons
Of my 'fate'

And lives as long,
As my stars can trace."

"I disagree," the first angel boasts
with light. "I disagree

With your disvalue of love.
With what esteem
Do you shame & weaken
This seed, which first flowered
Into infantine humanity?

Was it hate, this weapon
You justify with praise,
That which nurtured
The birth of progress?

Was it hate that united
Brothers & sons?
That bred kings
And marked countries & seas,
And fed healthy passions,
And rising charities?

Was hate that men valued
Consistently above self,

Was hate their light?

Does man count the stars,
And scour for hate?

Does he wake for hate?

To this you must agree,
It was 'Mother'

Love of country,
Of self, of companionship,
And immortality,

That nurtured our progress.

And my word,

'Mother'

Taught the trade of love
To members of progression—
So man has means to dream.

After all, aren't all dreams
Cultured by desire?

Desire nurtured by some love,

All love nurtured by 'Mother'

Mother nurtured by progress,

Progress nurtured
Back to desire...

And so the wheel
Of immortality spins.

The force behind my work,
Our constant word of

'Mother',

the ivory pillars

Of birth,

 Love and dreams."

Parable of the Snake

Beneath the falling business of winter
And half-covered skies
A farmer warm with family,
Still glowing from his brewed chai,
Still cushioned. Still soft—
Tends to the duty of his farm.

The old father quietly works a last chore
And digs his hands into the ice.
Nothing lives under such static
Chill, he thinks. *Only death can partner such life.*

As if his musings traced upon a mystery
He eyes a coiled shadow bedded
Within a sleeve of snow.
The floral spirals of his pattern, blue
With porcelain dust. Sleeping or dying. Or both.
All the weaponry of this snake's nature
Broken or stolen by furious wind's hand
And he lays, still sleeping. Or dying.

One to never leave the vulnerable
Into the blinded sights of fate,
The old farmer scoops the frozen
Remains of spirit into one hand,
With the other, wiping away any last edge
Of hate from his new friend's scales:

You will thank me for this when you thaw with love,
You will learn this form in your skin called care
And you will carve my will out of duty and truth,
This is my fatherly gift to you.

The mist of his words
Touch this crisp defeat;
A business of rebirth stirs.
The farmer smiles, knowing,

And welcomes the snake into his home.

The snake, long silenced, slowly strengthens
Into gentle content. He eats, and sleeps
And slips his long measure
Into the family's company and routine.

He thaws with every love the farmer could give.
He feasts on their delicacies, and spoils
Himself onto their warmest couch,
Soft and sleeping, growing. Smiling.
He is an extension of familiar care,
The very decorum of life.

Soon flowers and spring furnish the home,
The children have grown a lot this year and dance
In the moving parade of youth a little wiser.
The wife joins the newfound celebration, smiling,
And the father is alone in content—warm and busy.

And it is this very night that tests all love,
And all title and virtue in the old farmer
And his friend, the snake—

His words rise over the lilied breeze:

I saved you. I saved you.
I brought you life, once stolen--you were betrayed,
And I your charity. I taught you love, dear son.
I nourished the language of caring and feeding
And nursing body and spirit. Have you learned
Nothing from me, Sad Spirit?
Have you learned but hate of the basest form?

The quiet snake, crowned fat and powerful,
Lifts his entire shining frame of venomous majesty,
Nearing the old farmer's slowing expression.
His long pupils alert and black, measuring his attack.

"I fed you, and now you feast on me?" The farmer whispers.

The snake muses on his caretaker's fright, and as his nature
Would beckon, his tongue slips into truth:

"I never asked you to save me as you claim,
As good as you are, I am still the snake—

I am still hungry and my blood is still cold."

Quiet Thickening

It happens suddenly—
Between coffee and smiles.
Folded in busy language
Rises a quiet thickening—a moment
Swelling against the barriers of attention.

First it calls like a wind, an alerting
Breath. An altering pause—and you stare
Deep inside the faces of your companions
And you instead find a story, a muse.
Between sips they lose you—
They want prose, advice
You search for a pen, a memory—
A scent to recount your daily genius,

A napkin perhaps. Anything to write
And collect this intruding tone,

      Baking your day into a poem.

Vienna

Vienna's yellow palace rests above a cloud
Of chilled Hungarian lights,
But the gardens are still red and violet;
The three rocks still carry my wishes
From springtides before.
The snow still shines like a field
Of angel satin dressing history.

The garden maze of frosted Sylvester
Chills my worries solid;
That I may break myself
Apart and away and twirl
Like winter dust, my joy,
Clear above the rounded hills.

This Vienna! My love letter
To her time will ride the
Syllables of drawn memories
Into fields and museums,
Cathedrals, and music and smiles,
Swans dressed as ballerinas.

My Vienna, my youth
Of clouded breaths, and mittens
And *Herr Weihnachtsmann* the blushing giant
Offering chocolate upon chocolate on Christmas Eves.
The mornings after, my golden *schnitzels*
And toasted chestnuts and steaming punch and walks
Through *Stephansplatz*.

Her Sunday bells call forth an art
Of celebrated Strauss and violins
And tall maestros
(Lean measures of physical music)
All giants, all play in my heart.
I cradle the dream in my ear.

This beauty I possess with time
Calls through me like a river
Physical in all its glory,
Raising swans and lilies over the shore
And I let the river—a network of Europe
Work and flow through the veins
Of my memory and pride
And with one frothy sigh,
        I let the blue Danube
        Finally escape my eyes.

Unsere Zeit

Erinnere dich

Unserer Worte
Unserer Versöhnung
Unserer freundlichen Zeiten.

Etwas funkelt
Etwas regt sich sachte
Auf deinem Gesicht.

Wenn Zeit kommt und flüchtig vergeht,
Spiele ich mit deinem Kummer
Wie mit einem Kinderspiel.

Our Time

Recall

Our word,
Our relief,
Our friendly season.

Something glistens,
Something lightly plays
Upon your face.

When time comes and readily leaves,
I toy with your torment
Like a plaything.

Kinderspiel

Ich sehe dich, mein Schatz.
Deine Hand schmeigt sich
Innerhalb meiner
Stumm und klein.

Im Garten
In den Farben
In den bunten, kleinen Märchen
Reiche ich dir
Meine Hand.

Und zusammen
Jagen wir
Deine Sonne.

Children's Play

I see you, my sweet.
Your hand folds
Into mine,
Still and small

In the garden,
In the colors,
In the gleaming and small fairytales
I give my hand
To you.

And together,
We chase
Your sun.

永生之光

一道永生之光，揭开了一线黎明。
再道永生之光，蕴含了些许思绪。
这太阳之火啊，
燃烧了这个爱的季节！

Immortal Light

One immortal light, a little dawn
Two immortal lights, a little thought
Fire upon the sun
This is the season of love.

Eidolons

A conversation with the sea.

The friendly sea said unto me:

You ask of what I dream
When higher colors glint and peel?
I dream of airy callings, sweet and clear,
Laughing stars and echoed fates,
And shattered liquid
On my shore, rounding
As one orb, and one eidolon,
One soft and folding muse.

You ask of what I feel
When hardened eyes hook
And reel before my gaze?
I laugh but one starry tune, one
Charred and healing dawn,
An iron valve of song,
Hallow and deep and full
One orb, one eidolon
In which you pray.

You ask of what I sing?
I sing for thee, I pray in quakes
I glint of glass and polished
Feat. Pearly muse, thoughtful prayer,
        I give and take your dreams.

Exist

Nobody sleeps in the theater
Of dreams. The world is wild,
With the deficits of absorption.

Always something to carve,
To draw, to pull, and claw, and care
Always a tear, a constellation, a creamy
Sigh. Always the breadth of a city,

The blinking theater of lights,
Sinking in the vacancies of night.

Always an attention to tie our
Muses—It is what we
Do with natural skill,

To exist on many planes
To exist in opal colors.

It is in the natural artistry
Like breathing. Like laughing.

To exist like violet thunder
Muted by its entrance.

To exist
Like the soft lily,
Hidden

Among the thriving.
Among the weeds
Of hunters.

To exist like the shining paint
On a canvas

Awake for 2000 years.
To exist, dear embracer;

To exist with no pardon.
To utterly exist like the poem
That lives long past its words.
          It is what we do with natural skill.

Truth in Beauty

What esteem cradles a poet's virtues?
I have yet to weigh wealth in his discoveries.
I do believe a poet is a lonely collector,
Tied intrusively into a world his letters adorn.
A certain seeker, clothed in eloquence—
Waving truth in every beauty,
And beauty in every truth.

If he were a magician, with the wake
Of a word, rising beauty from a void,
Molding truths into shapes unfamiliar
Or solely cued by his own reasoning,
Owning beauty. Owning Colors.
Does he become a thief? He takes
What is ours, and unfolds in gifts...
Or a ray of God...
And we commend him
For these treasures he unearths,
For creating this beauty, and all her sights
And journeys later tied to our sleep.

But, in truth, he shaped none such beauty
Since beauty first shaped him.
And all the virtues in his name
Lose their celebrated wings,
And he is no thief, nor ray.
He is a breather
And he dwells among the rest.
A breather, a man
Who chases beauty,
Cups her, and presents her
Under a certain worship,
And charms our sensory faiths.
He is the beauty in our truths.

The Trillium

Poetry:

The early evening star
The muse of three ivory words
Tied to one gravity of reason—
Tied to the gold pollen
Of birth and rebirth and rebirth.

The trillium and all her creamy luck
Equal in truth—unbiased, measured, even
And blooming silver on all three faces
Of muse. Serving sincerity
On all three plates of heaven.
The trio of weakness, wisdom, clarity
Paralleling the blonde expressions
Of stars—and the outstretched
Limbs of stars—
Blooming and bedding against
A warm cliff—Soft on a poetic
Landscape; unfolding
On a precipice,
Leaning clear
Over its
Demise:

Poetry,

    The Trillium.

Sincerity

For Ramzi

It is the poetry in your stare
That which calls forth
All my sense and muse.

I could write your features
Into a fine line, you know.

Your hair

I could recite beyond the bend

The chin, beyond the cleft.

I know both well—
Through art and mind

The build of a man ever

Present

I can truly recount
With my embrace.

The form of another

Measure

I can touch with equal
Poetry

As you had touched me.

I can breathe with equal muse
And stirring sincerity.

Celestial Rumors

Last night the stars
Rumored of his defeat.
They lined a perfect
Smile across
The navy duress
And shined a mocking
Tale of every destiny
He had disowned...

He was given the rights
To happiness—
And yet he had baffled
Even the gods.

What is it that he
Didn't deserve?
What promises tied his story
To the successions of failure?

And will they mock him?
Will destiny dilate
Its mirror upon his faded pride
And reflect the face of past
Fears?

Will his faith fold, slowly
Piece by happy piece
Into the darkest chapters
Of his world? Will He
Release the hope he was gifted,
The sandy world he had quickly built
With dreams?

How quiet the night seems.

He refuses to search the presence of stars
He refuses to recount their promise;
        They have already deceived him once.

Alien Nation

What is left to say about good isolation?
What can I mark as my own reflection,
Without intruding on another poet's muse?

How can I plow my journey to lands
Alien to everyone, including myself?

Private lands, like cornered nations in this globe
With protruding thoughts and moons recalling my muse—

In this private darkness lined with sleeping homes
Warm in candlelight, a thinker dwelling inside—
On this solid muse where the traveler meets the path
Later tied to his journeys and written truth
I trace its shadows of living green with my mind

As I scour the long silent street,
Waiting for my thoughts.

I stand—a spinning thinness surrounding me,
And I peer, alone, upon a giant amber ship
We can call the city moon—waiting
To take me in.

I lift my curiosity above the friendly glow
And search his darker half
We're always drawn
To the comforts—the extensions
Of ourselves in others.

I think.
And even in my alien land of mediations
I stand alone. Waiting alone, peering deep
Past the concrete desert of speculations;
No sigh elevates to enjoy this sight.

Personally, I wouldn't invite just anyone—

This is my nation, my crafting of humor and rest.
I am my own alien in this nation—always a stranger.
Always a visitor. A traveler journeying through--
Dangerous to be otherwise...

And even in my secrecy—I seek
A sweeter truth to undress
A treat welcomed nowhere else but here...

And when I celebrate this given truth—
I celebrate in my loyal land of cerebration
Where the streets are thin
And the world is tight around me—
Accepting this prose
I create half humorously
With a taste and manner I formed
While in momentary musing in
          My darling Alien Nation.

Currency of Love

Love. The word...
You're as changing, constant
As stories and art
Beneath the stones of age.
A beautiful muse

Dare I say?

You are the spoken to—
The listening star
Ever present
Ever truthfully there
Sleeping in pockets of sighs
And fantasies
Illimitable. Unreachable
To the basest of men.
Still unattainable
To the truly intellect.

You are the accrescence
Of letters and prose
And valued streams of expressions
Meeting like wild rivers into the sea.
You are the element in every rhyme.

Dare I say more?

You are the glistening.
The muse. Always the muse
If nothing else—
You are the lyric of insanity
And electricity of obsession.
You sing of human angels bound to earth
Tied to the sights of admirers
You are the heat in their wounds
Striking and piercing
Well into their dreams

If nowhere else.

You are the ungotten,
The mystery in every class
Valued. Above life.
You are the volatile economy
Wavering on the ropes of bankruptcy
Unsettled in your victim's wealth.

I Heard Songs From Widows

I.

I heard songs from widows,
Heavy tunes. Heavy.
Plaiting their ribbons of sorrow
Into night. Into night.

I heard their death and prayers
And stars. I touched their stars.
I heard songs from widows,
And kissed their lonely child.

I watched and waited
As they do...
Facing their sea
Of rolling time.
Promising times
Of no return.

Promised times
They learned to forgive.

Forgive your hopes
Songstress. Forgive
The ebbing rivers of your heart
Pouring hope

And love heavy
Past your folded hands,
Your folded lips,
And through your folded eyes.

Forgive the monster sea,
Dear widow.

His war is no match to the master
Of your faith.

He does what he is taught,
Rolling, rising, breaking.

He is taught to ride
The deaths of your pride.

II.

The sea quilts with silent battles,
Such force met with the waiting widow.
Her smile as slow as the tides, rising.
She tunes her patience with stormy petrel songs
And here she accompanies hope,
Warm, in her blanket of dreams,
Eyeing the sea, the husband,
And its dilating possibilities.

And here the sea returns her smile
Chanting her husband's name,
His path, his joy, his victories.
Rising and rolling and breaking,
Polishing his name like a spear
Straight through her hopes.
And she cries.

The Light of You

And in the brightest night
Emerges into the human heat
That enlarged thought:

Light of nights know
A vow more brilliant.

I draw an intimacy with the stars,
You sigh a promise on my lips.
A strange entangled mass
Of luminous limbs and fingers--
A river filled with stars.
The birds light on the branches
and dawn pulls me away.
I am torn at the seams.
The essentially broken poetry
of my loving motions halted
at your breath.
You ask for a vow returned.
My love is not mine to give.
I escape the light of any promise:
I have loved you
With indifference
By omission of dreams.

Amore Vulgare

The love story of Venus and Mars

Verbs of passion
Catch onto fallen swords
And twined daisies.
The new atlas
Of rivers and sighs
Bind this journied night—
One scene of two iron deities
Caught inside their love
And war.

Hidden beneath sights
And loyalties of duties

Two stony myths
In their palace of starry hours
Explore deepest revenge
In moral breadth
And praise the gods
In harmony
For this quaking gift
Of heat upon heat
And lies upon love.

The beautiful
And un-dividing
Tribute and crowing
To *Amore Vulgare*

The Triangle

He loves me the way
A net loves the bird:
A quick filling
A quicker escape—
The loud cast of his seductions
Meets my flight of air.

But she loves him...
Tying her attentions
To him—his breath
And pursuit for challenge
Fixed with her care—

Her graceful fingers
Adoring his frays
And mending the knots
To strengthen the net
He casts for me.

Only Child

I hardly walked as a child.
Like a spider I clung to her;
Attaching myself to a skirt,
A hand, a moment of guilt—
Anything to bring me up
Above the floor. I never
Resisted to weakness.
My frowns could move
The Alps. A single tear
And quivering chin
Was an earthquake
In my mother.
I was an only child,
And my release
Was in my mother's arms.

Comedy

Your laughter sinks
Into a special violence,
Into truth and beards
And your stories wander...

Gyrating about our smiles,
Not a poison, not a spear,
A simple wind that lifts
Our spirits of esteem.

It is your skill
Your celebrated skill,
To own disappointment,
To pluck the thorns
That scratched your heart for years,
It is your skill
To draw our laughers of relief
From the therapy of your wounds.

As the weight of performance
Falls on your gestures,
Your lofty gestures of distress
Abandonment hatred greed
We laugh in tune
So you may find
Warmth of pride
Beneath this heavy past
Your fortune calls from you.

Winter Promises Spring

If winter should release his ghosts
One then all, one snow then death—
If all our flights of birds and song
Leave with winter's hand—
And all the lyrics of our dreams
Leave in tune with fears.

We round our cheers of rosy tides:
"Winter parts for spring!"

We call for frost to pass his game,
Though hours chill through May
We pray in warm and lonely sighs,
Within the musings of our day,

We call upon this spell of time
As winter's claws unite
In dance that breeds more winter,
Outside a groaning night.

High and long, they stretch and dive,
And breathe more souls with ice.
They strike the bending tree,
Black with bitten fright.

When starry fields of wonderland
Are hardened by their pride,
They spot a rosy promise,
Silenced in their ice.
There, they curiously gather,
Like a circle of smiling kings ...

Winter parts for spring.

A Ma Mère: Lullabies

For Chandani and Izzat

Moth tap
Of momma's heart,
A star upon his cheek,
A chin pressed
Upon his curls...
A mother cradles
His peace to sleep.

The calm integrity
Of solid night
Where nightingales
Delight in play,
Over the braided
Work of mother
And child.

The intimate hum
Of company...
All lullabies
Of the heart.

Sun: The Winter Siren

It is light without heat.
High and pale;
Vivid as the irised
Stars on earth;

Today, she is our empress,
Wild with winter,
Winking among the jewels of snow,
Musing art without the touch.

High above the presence
Her Sereneness tunes
An embrace with satin limbs:
An open stage of warmth and treats.
A curtain, a throne of cosmos,
An air of infinity.

And through theses waves
She sings of static pleasantries.

Upon this winter sky and sea,
A songstress preens
With crowned,
And hollowed dignity.

Moon: The Sun's Sister

Poor ivory maiden,
Your beauty is not your own.

This light upon your flesh
A broken portrait
Of rivers and tides.
A gilded memory,

Are you pale with muse,
Relieving a narrow river of lamentations
Onto the sea of our company?

A quiet roll across the world,
Friendless and aching;
A rocky shell of all that was light and joy

And you are gone.

Lonely Autumn

The festive sun is far from me,
Heavy but far. Never reaching me.
Spring is busy, a birth I cannot touch.
As I rush through the values
Of the wind and ride her hidden songs,
I delight in coolness pressing the sun.
I breathe for autumn,
For the snapping of spring,
And her pearls of days strung together
By birth, beginnings, ribbons. A parade
Of new love and trumpets.
Delightful and loud...

How I run from spring,
That I may find a single tree,
A silhouette of tamed loneliness
Dark with cognizance, aged
With autumn's coins.
Where I may hang my company,
And wrap my cool spirit upon his thoughts.
Where I may braid colors of friendship
Onto his bared and broken branches,
And find eternal values in a quiet thought.

The Study of a Soul

An Apparition

Caught. Woven
In delicate dawn—
In wide peace, I hear
A warm invasion of eyes.

A frosted complexion
Unseen – known,
Like one knows a smile
Streaming through the tangled
Universes of doubt.

Quiet and heavy, it waits
In a precise corner beside
The bed.

A whispered weight
And time slows
Like honey. Like a prayer.

I wait in thickening
Silence. I wait, then ask:
Do I have your blessing?

An answer lifts
And bows low
Inside my sighs.
I open my eyes:

Yes, I say and rise.

I Deny the Muse

I deny the isolation:
The poem
The muse
The knowing
And the serene lace
Of morals and philosophy.
The string of moments
Polished like pearls
Rolling against my flesh

I deny the sensation
Take it far from my will.
Divide the extension
Of measures and truth
Sprouting
Five corners.

I deny you, isolation
Do you hear my prayer?
I deny the fine work
Of *visio beatifica*
Stirring and living
Inside the letters
Inside my views.

If I am weakened
And pulped to forbidden
I deny the scales
In which to measure all truths.
And so away with muse
The light to the eventual letter.
Away with the reminder
That I am no better.

The Lullaby

Love surrender,
Swaying splendor,
Softly mend your aching cry.

With fragile joy,
A twilight boy,
Lifting songs and blessings high

To keep you warm
From aging storms
With a tender, knowing eye,

And draw you near
In humble sphere
Through a rosy
Summer sky.

To One Poet

What fire fills your mouth
To speak of the hottest truth?
Was it a right? A virtue—a serene
Acceptance that you are the sister
Of the greatest god
Walking here on earth?
Constituting the earth;
Spilling your wisdom to men
Who have no souls? You say people
Never have souls, nor existence,
Nor appreciation for your gifts
As the caretaker. They should be filled
With your love by now—balloons
Of wisdom, spirits full of truth
And seeds, but they failed you--
And you recite this knowledge
So that they may learn
What is blinding acceptance;
Even then you're doubtful
That they have minds to understand...
You have your words, your rhyme
Your virtue
To ride their worth
Clear above the trees
And living moon
You open heaven to enlighten,
Enlighten and devour
Their measure.
And you watch smiling
As your knowledge
Of their basest form
Finally burns their soul
With the embers of your work.

Our Touch

My darling, it is in our touch—
In our softest joy. Our fingers gracefully
Sing the textures of love
Our flowering muse in speech,
All colors of berries and stars.
It is in our prayer with summer lips
Which tears apart the seams
Of fate-- and one lilting star
Brightens our hair—falling
Slowly between our embrace.

To Love You

I never chose to love you
Against the grain of my own existence.

It was your lips, ripe as season's berries,
That which I bit and drank.

It was the world I chose to surrender to.
It was the world I found in you.

Will you come back, bright as air
And surrender your tides of lies?

Will you return your shallow touch
And break the sun with sky?

I Cannot Sleep

The restless muse to write at 2AM

I cannot sleep. I cannot sleep!
My mind hangs
Upon the window pane
And catches the paler winter night
And all her forgotten stars
Lost and constant. But lost!

And so I hang my musings
Over my head—a dream catcher,
A braided work of skill— decorated
With blue imagery and lazy pearls.

I cannot sleep. I cannot sleep!
Outside, the iris yawns!

And all her lighter muse
Frosting my window pane bright!
Winking stars! A mirror here on Earth.
All fate and cosmos...
Busy and bound!

See? I will not sleep
Until I tie their values
On a page, and catch
Their world in a sigh—
Until I master and tame
The spirit of their flight...
And pull their mask of chill aside.

I cannot sleep. I cannot breathe!
I cannot steer these story wings!

I tug apart my knotted musing
And all her polished luck...
And release the cosmos from my grip.

(Earthly and Divine)
I unhook the silver night from my thoughts,
And unbraid the daedal wind.

Beneath a setting dust of patience,
Hushed and light,
I fall asleep with all my peace.

Ode to Shakespeare

As precise as our finest line in art
And as pretty as a picture in memory
Painting a scene so lovely
One truly does wonder if
All the world's a stage.

But the characters have the limbs
Of veins and sunlight
And the slow grace of clouds.
The conversation of wings—
The laughter of waves
High and low, with the frothing
Of winter in spring.

All the world's an art
As green and burgundy
As the truest mermaid and her fin.
As dark as its bobbing crystal
Raising busy imaginations.

All the world's a moment
A pretty canvas to our wisdom
A darling shift of truth.
A haunting.

A stage.

And each must play its part.

Watching Adam Heal

A 20/20 special on a healer

Hole of pain
Of illness. Filling
A seamless rescue
From your friendly prayers—
And fixed companions feasting
On your grace. A special melody
For the soul, a hand to god.

Beneath the physiology of hope,
Basking in fluorescent hours of hymn
Tracing the auras, your hands
Clasp the invisible bloodless cancers
Tumors binding the heart
You tremble and fix the open wounds.
It is in your fingers, the dance
Of meditation—

Eyes open, prayers flared
Dreams woven into a story
And solidarity cries:

A miracle

A true and utter healing
Of belief.

Two Halves of My Dream

The night sky casts a shining tale
To recognize the dream tracing clearly
A person I know,
Consciously.

It is the familiar face I see round
In all its suggestion—expression
Of the slowest love, I dare
Never recall outside my
Careful thoughts.

It is the vertigo of something
Later recaptured—
The look, the muted muse
Before me, while I am only awake

And the dawning breaks above me
And folds over me a warm truth.
I can only smile, warm in my secrecy.

My two halves woven
Into a seamless whole

When I dream.

And I can only smile.

Unveiling

The splinters of her heart
Guided her home
Through the quiet snow
Through the calm
And loud machinery
Of something lost.

The world tastes metallic
Today. Iron. Cold.
Paled and stinging
A staleness

She runs to escape—
An expression chilled
To her every muse
Every fiber of distrust

Aching her lungs.
She dares not breathe.

She found him today
Though she wishes she hadn't.
She found the truth
Inside their deepest embrace.

It was the lie she had wanted.
A woven pride
To hold together her world:
A little denial to mend her soul.

Optimism / Pessimism

I do recall to smile and fly
When luck rides the astral tides.
My cheeks high, my story bright,
I do, I do recall to smile.

When happy spheres release
Their hinges, I do receive their world.
When sunlight bakes my whispers,
I do recount the joy.

But to every light there is a haunting,
To every sincerity, its truth,
To every happiness there is a pause
Of black and sadness,
To every world, a balanced view.

The First Concert

What's one big love affair?
A halo of music colors your curls;
You strum our spirits
Above our heads.
Stirring a melody
Of our sighs
Like a smiling lover
Outside our sins.

Your darker measure tied
To the wall idolizing
Your shoulders
And we sing your words,

The chorus of our worship
Drawn and low,
Our eyes shine on you
Like a sea

Of flickering fires,
Your hand lifts to our silence.
And we pause...
Then you smile

And we sing for you.
How we sing for you.
This easy command
You draw from us...
Your motions electric
To our nerves
And we become human
Switches, conductors of your
Musical breadth,
Valued rings of transferred energy
To your songs.
Switch us off and we pause to sigh,
With a wave, we raise the values

Of your words, through our rounded lips
Above the air of common sweat,
Past your smile,
And over a throne we crafted for you.

Hatred

Hatred, I pity you.
Simple, raging child.
You have been used
And misused

And tossed and abandoned
In what we do not know.

And worked to despair
As faded tears
Wasted on the shifting seas
Of what we do not
Understand.

Hatred, you are the practice
Of fear, and the prayer
For blind souls.

Strip this warm glinting robe
Braided with the threads of our lofty
And loud impatience,
Peel this flesh
Of our vulgar misunderstandings,
Bake this busy tongue
Of envy bound to us all.

And what then isolates your word?

Hatred, the finite misnomer,
I truly, and utterly pity you,
For you have one home,
And one voice.

Sad Hatred, lost orphan—
Stripped bare of existence—
I can only love you,
And with one gentle sigh—
You exist no more.

Crossing Stars

Poetry recounts the slender sigh
Long and unbroken, once the routine
Of breathing is taught—

Watching stars cross, colliding two fates,
Watching compassion storm into Armageddon—
Into a shining path of sighs
And worries and time. Poetry—that is.

The poet watches the eye
Of every storm. The gray hair.
The sleeping child beneath her parent's door.

The Living Air

> *America's early years*

Within the valves
Of louder years
We strike and pray
And weld our fears.

We storm and seek
And plough and reach;
We die and bind and rise
While heaven swallows
Our plumes of pride.

We happy crew,
We unformed muse,
We braze and weld
And pound and die,
And rise again,
Our blessings high;

We move as one,
One wind,
One strike -
We lance as one
Across the sky,

We pound one song
One rhyme of peace,

As we rise
Above

The tides!

Shadow

My shadow folded unto me –
My dear friend of servitude,
How you frighten me!

Picnic

The sun tumbles low above our toasts
And we break the honesty of summer
With our kisses, hearts, happy surprises.
Our sitting patience, a clockwork love story,
The tolls of waves roll hour by hour
But we've woven the fibers of time
So tightly, so securely, with such passion,
Time is but time. All time, a uniform
Of constant company and energy.
A long and unbroken service to our joy.

The summer waves may tire, the sun may roll
Across the orb like a shining tribute
Framing our steady smiles and truth,
The stars may vary their presence
Above our heads; beneath this changing
Promise, beneath this pulsing symphony
Of predicted melody and lights, our picnic
Of summer sandwiches and ruby cherries will cast
All the moons and suns out of orbit,
Out of our personal tale. And beneath
The web of stars, our hearts' journeys
Will settle fast inside the eye of spinning
Summer and hurricanes of truth.

Hardest to Forgive

My heart wants
A metaphor—
Loud and wide
And limitless,
A long river of confidence
(A virtuoso of love)
To ride inside you,
And through you
As it fills through me.
Changing me.
A beautiful
Metaphor
Locked
Inside
My
Skin.

My blood
Swirls for you
Deep into the stems
And limbs of frozen grammar.
My grammar unhinged
From my intellect
And calm
The basest
Form
I cover
Quietly.

My heart speaks
For you. How she
Recites into the deepest
Hours the laws and penalties
Of your charm. My lips
Fastened shut
Swollen
With

Everything
When I touch you

So to not shame
The measure
Of our
Company

With the
Speech
Hardest
To forgive.

Charity of Spring

A mother robin nesting against our windowpane

My feathered pet of spring
Greets us with one shining
Eye, black as the night is night,
Round as the constant moon,
Starry -- like a brimming sigh.

Framed upon the window pane,
She holds her home of three
And through the warmth and cool
Of day, she fluffs and preens and feeds
Three warm integrities of spring.

Day by day, she greets and stirs
And plays against the glass.
A happy plump of heaven's grace,
She chimes of hope, of love.

Thank you for this cycled art,
This charity of spring,
This daily feeding in our hearts
This promise
      Of fidelity.

The Chained Hills

The night is empty,
Its sky clean—
Like glass speared
Into an open fate

The chained hills,
Are shrugged in snow,
Shaded in pockets of futurity-

One golden ray weaves
Their distance to mine
And I wait,
Isolated in prayer,
For my future to reach my joy.

The Watching Gravestones

To my left
Grey pearls
Line perfectly
Between the flowers.
I cannot see them –
The remembered names,
Little carved dates,
Though silently their fates
Watch me
Pass through
Unknown memories,

Rows of unblinking
Eyes fixed
To my every
Breath,

Like a painting
Frozen in glory
Watching, breathing, alive

In fixed wonderment.

Ratio and Voluntas

Ratio
Voluntas
Divide the soul.

A constituted muse
Fixed and intractable
Overmasters the present
With two songs.
The future is bare
While the moon caged
By its own reflection

Claws deeper into the sea.

Human Nature

The wind had been bred to lace
The rivalries of spring
Into innumerable songs of motion.

The moon pressed a look into the sky,
And all bent into one portrait of Justice
Moved by men.

Let Us Love Again

Let us trace the lifted
Smile; the lips of the
Remembered.

Let us retrieve again
The memories of a forgotten child
Dying of abandonment,
His spirit hungry to be realized.

Let us recall again,
Even for a moment,
The sting of desertion
Inside the shadow
Of a disappearing boy.

Let us catch
The faint prefiguring glimmer
Of a spirit filling with praise,

We have been created to love
And be loved.
Let us never forget.

Because this deprived spirit is molded with the same
Hand. With the same stroke,
And the same love
Our god molded our measure to the world:

The hungry woman, the quiet child, the leper,
The good, the wealthy, and the poor. the misguided
And the abandoned.

Let us remove some suffering
From this world; let us offer a piece of bread,
A cup of water,

And if we are to carry one resolution in our hearts as
Human beings, as portraits of a higher compassion,

Let this promise be:

    I will love again.

Mother Theresa's Meditations

Mother Theresa's Meditations

English Translations

I.

Gjej Kohë

Find Time

Find time for thought—it is the source of power.
Find time for prayer—it is our world's most virtuous
potential.

Find time for laughter—it is music for the soul.

Find time for play—it is the mystery of youth.
Find time for love—it is Heaven's gift
Find time for benevolence—it is the absolute happiness

Find time to read—it is the well of knowledge.
Find time to befriend—it is the path to joy.
Find time to work—it is the promise for our future.

Find time for goodwill—it is the key
To Heaven.

II.

Jeta

Life

Life is a possibility, embrace it.
Life is beautiful, admire it.
Life is wonderful, enjoy it.
Life is a dream, follow it.
Life is bewilderment, face it.
Life is a mission, fulfill it.
Life is a game, play it.
Life is a gem, cherish it.
Life is rich, savor it.
Life is lovely, revere it.
Life is a mystery, profess it.
Life is pain, endure it.
Life is a song, sing it.
Life is a tragedy, carry it.
Life is luck, benefit from it.
Life is an adventure, be regardful of it.
Life is very precious, delight in it.
Life is a war, learn from it.
Life is life, fight for it.

III.

Poezia

The Poem

Release me, oh Lord,
From the desire to be adored,
From the desire to be exalted,
From the desire to be honored,
From the desire to be applauded,
From the desire to be elevated,
From the desire to be sought after for advice,
From the desire to be commended,
From the desire to be famous,
From the fear of being disdained,
From the fear of being disparaged
From the fear of being denounced
From the fear of being repellent
From the fear of being forgotten
From the fear of being mocked,
From the fear of being suspicioned!
Amen.

Mother Theresa's Meditations on Joy, Love, and Faith

IV.

A joyful heart is the inevitable result
Of a heart burning with love.
Joy is not the reflection of a personality;
It is increasingly difficult to appear cheerful:
This is one more reason to achieve happiness
And to fill our hearts.

Joy is prayer, joy is strength, joy is love.
He gives more who gives with joy.

To the children and the poor,
To all who suffer and are alone,
Always offer a kind smile;
Do not only give your care, but give your heart as well
The opportunity to offer more is rare
But joy is abundant and everlasting
Like waves rippling from a heart filled with love.
If you encounter difficulties in your work
Accept this with joy,
With a smile. In this, others will follow your good work.
And the best path to show your gratitude
Lies in the acceptance of all things connected with joy.

If you are covered with joy, joy will shine
Through your eyes and in your view,
In your speech and your discipline.
However deeply buried, joy will break apart the will.

Joy is contagious.
Seek then to surround yourself with joy
Wherever you go.

V.

Joy is the presence of an angel in our life.
It is the virtue of a generous spirit
Sometimes it is a cloak that covers
this life of sacrifice, but you have to feel this emotion.
A man who possesses this gift, often reaches
The top of the mountain
And shines like the sun on the bay of society.

VI.

Acts of love
Are works of peace.
Every time you share
Your love with others
You will notice peace
Doubling between you.
Where there is peace, there is God,
And so pour peace and joy, God,
In our hearts.

VII.

The gravest disease at present
Is to feel unwanted,
To feel abandoned.
There are so many people in the world
Who die of hunger,
But still more people die
From lack of love.
Every being needs love.
Every being should know
This desire,
Is important to God.

VIII.

Mos jeto kurrë pa jetë!

Do not ever live without life!

The most beautiful day? Today.
The biggest obstacle? Fear.
The easiest act? To stumble.
The gravest failure? To give up.
The root of all evil? Egoism.
The best distraction? Work.
The worst route to follow? Cowardliness.
The best teachers? Children.
The deepest primal need? Communication.
The highest honor? To be useful to others.
The greatest mystery? Death.
The worst defect? A sour temper
The most dangerous being? The liar.
The most wretched feeling? Resentment.
The most beautiful gift? Forgiveness.
The most indispensable? Family.
The quickest path? The moral way.
The greatest comfort? Inner peace.
The most sincere welcome? The smile.
The best remedy? Optimism.
The greatest pleasure? Accomplishment.
The greatest force? Faith.
The most valuable friends? Servants of God.
The most beautiful of all? Love.

Masiela Lusha is an award-winning actress, author, and humanitarian.

Lusha gained recognition as a poet at the age of twelve. While learning English as her fourth language, Lusha published her first book of poetry, *Inner Thoughts*. This feat determined Lusha as the youngest author in the world to publish a book in English and Albanian. By the age of fifteen, Lusha graduated from high school and published her second book of poetry, *Drinking the Moon*. At eighteen, Lusha was accepted as a junior at the University of California Los Angeles. Among other notable work, Lusha has translated Albanian poems and prayers by Mother Theresa, and has written several poems in German.

As an award-winning actress, Lusha appeared in over 20 films and television projects. She is best known for her portrayal of Carmen Lopez in Warner Brother's globally syndicated series, *George Lopez*, and for her portrayal of Sharon in Sony Picture's *Blood: The Last Vampire*.

Throughout her career, Lusha was appointed ambassador to a number of international charities including the World Assembly of Youth, Sentebale, Uncommon Good and Athgo International. Lusha also established her own charity, Children of the World.

Lusha earned an English degree from the University of California Los Angeles, and currently resides in Los Angeles, California with her husband, Ramzi.

Made in the USA
Monee, IL
07 July 2026